LIVING WITH
BLINDNESS

Patsy Westcott

RAINTREE

Titles in the series
Living with Asthma
Living with Blindness
Living with Cerebral Palsy
Living with Deafness
Living with Diabetes
Living with Down Syndrome
Living with Epilepsy
Living with Leukemia

Published by Raintree Steck-Vaughn Publishers, an imprint of Steck-Vaughn Company

Library of Congress Cataloging-in-Publication Data
Westcott, Patsy.
Living with blindness / Patsy Westcott.
     p.   cm.—(Living with)
     Includes bibliographical references and index.
     Summary: Explains the condition of blindness, its possible causes, and how it affects the everyday lives of those who are dealing with it..
     ISBN 0-8172-5741-1
     1. Blindness—Juvenile literature.
     [1. Blind. 2. Physically handicapped.]
     I. Title. II. Title: Blindness
     RE52.W47 1999
     617.7'12—dc21   98-32230

Printed in Italy. Bound in the United States.
1 2 3 4 5 6 7 8 9 0 03 02 01 00 99

Picture acknowledgments
The publishers would like to thank: John Birdsall 21; Getty Images/Alan Bedding 23, /Will and Deni McIntyre 20; Science Photo Library/Argentum 10 (both), 11 (both), /Bsip Edwige 24, /Hank Morgan 20; John Walmsley 8, 22, 30; Wayland Picture Library cover (bottom right), 9, /Angus Blackburn cover (top left), 29, /Martyn F. Chillmaid title page, 4 , 5 (both), 6, 12, 13, 14, 15, 16 (both), 17, 19, 26, 27, 29, /Angela Hampton cover (main picture), 18. The illustration on page 7 is by Kevin Jones Associates. Special thanks to Barbara Shalit for all the work she did on this book.

Contents

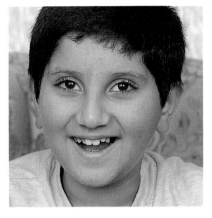

Meet Mathar, Lucy, and Katie

Mathar is ten years old. He is blind. And he does not hear well. Mathar lives with his mom and dad, his brother, Tom, and his sister, Nusrat. Tom can see, but Nusrat is also blind. Mathar could see until he was four years old, but now he can see only movement and shadows. He likes reading, playing on his computer, and going swimming with Tom and Nusrat.

▽ Mathar and his sister, Nusrat, are both blind.

Lucy is 15 years old. She is the oldest of five brothers and sisters. They all live at home with their mom and dad. Lucy goes to the same school as her brother Matthew. Lucy has been blind since she was born, so she has never known what it is like to be able to see. When she graduates from school, Lucy wants to be a computer programmer. She likes going shopping with her best friend Sophie and listening to music.

△ Lucy and Sophie listen to music in Lucy's bedroom.

Katie is partially sighted. Katie could see until she was a teenager. Now she cannot see out of the center of her eyes. If she moves her head, she can sometimes see out of the sides. Katie lives with her husband, Mike, and their two children, Sarah and Dominic, who are both in college. She works as a receptionist. For the last three years, Katie has had a guide dog named Teddy. Katie enjoys dancing, walking, and traveling.

▷ Katie's guide dog, Teddy, helps her get around.

What is blindness?

Blindness can mean many things. It usually means that some part of the eye, or even the brain, is damaged, resulting in partial or total loss of vision.

You may imagine that people who are blind live in a

world of complete darkness. This is not so. Most blind people can see something, but they see much less than people with perfect vision. A blind person may be able to see light from a window. He or she may be able to tell if a light is on in a room or if the light is switched off. A blind person may be able to see movement but not shape or form. He or she might see the same things, but what they see is all blurred and misty or in patches. Many blind people can see colors. Most blind people can see enough to recognize their friends and family if they stand close to them.

◁ Wearing glasses helps Mathar see outside in the sun. It is too dark inside buildings for him to see, even with his glasses on.

How we see

Our eyes work a bit like a camera.

1. We need light to see things. Light rays bounce off objects and enter our eyes first through the cornea, the clear, frontmost layer of the eyes and then through the pupil, a small black hole in the middle of the eye.

2. Inside the eye, the lenses focus the light rays, just as camera lenses do. This produces an upside-down, miniature image of whatever the eye is looking at. The image falls on the retina. In a camera, the upside-down image falls on the film.

3. The retina is a layer of tissue on the inside back wall of the eye. It has cells that turn the upside-down image into nerve impulses.

4. The electrical signals travel to the brain along a bundle of fibers called the optic nerve. It's a bit like electrical signals passing down a telephone wire.

5. The brain turns the signals into a three-dimensional (3-D) picture and turns it around so we see everything the right way up.

All this happens so quickly that you do not even know it is happening.

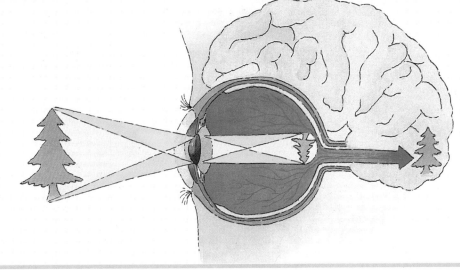

If someone is partially sighted, he or she can see more than someone who is totally blind but less than someone who is fully sighted. Another term used to describe people who are blind or partially sighted is "visually impaired."

Why are some people blind?

There are many reasons why people are blind or partially sighted. Some people are born blind, although this is rare. Others become blind as children or adults because of disease or accidents. There are about 40 million people in the world who are blind. One and a half million of them are children.

In developed countries, such as the United States, the UK, France, Australia, and Germany, most people who are blind are over 65 years old. Most of these people could see for most of their lives but lost their sight as they got older.

Some children and young people in these countries are also blind. Most of them were born blind or went blind in the first few weeks of their lives. Some of them have other difficulties such as deafness or learning disabilities.

▽ This blind girl has a special teacher to help her in school.

△ In poor countries, such as India, more children go blind.

In some developing countries, more children are blind because they do not get enough vitamin A. This is found in green leafy vegetables and in red and yellow fruits and vegetables. Some become blind because of diseases such as measles or diarrhea, which use up stores of vitamin A. Other children become blind because of accidents or lack of clean water.

Mathar and his sister, Nusrat, inherited a condition that causes blindness. When blindness is inherited, other members of the family might also be blind. Another example of inherited visual impairment is the condition Katie has, retinitis pigmentosa. This condition damages cells in the retina. Katie doesn't know anyone else in her family with retinitis pigmentosa, but her mother says one of her aunts had it.

Another condition, called glaucoma, can cause visual impairment. It happens when fluid pressure builds up in the eyeball. This damages the optic nerve. Medicine or surgery can keep glaucoma from getting worse, but they cannot repair the optic nerve. Some kinds of glaucoma can be inherited.

Some people become blind because of disease. In older people, a common cause of blindness is a disease called macular degeneration. In this condition, cells in the middle of the retina are damaged. This causes a "blind spot." The person with the condition may see things around the outside of their eye when he or she looks at something, but not in the middle.

△ Someone with macular degeneration might see a street in this way.

△ Someone with glaucoma might see a street in this way.

△ Someone with diabetic retinopathy might see a street in this way.

△ Someone with cataracts might see a street in this way.

Sometimes blindness is a result of a disease affecting some other part of the body. For example, some people with diabetes may develop a condition called diabetic retinopathy. This causes damage to the retina that may make their sight patchy and blurred.

Cataracts are a common cause of blindness all over the world. Cataracts make the lens of the eye cloudy, so light cannot enter it. People sometimes develop cataracts as they grow older. Or cataracts can be caused by injury to the eye. Cataracts are more common in sunny countries, such as India, because the amount of ultraviolet light from the bright sun is harmful to the sensitive surface of the eye.

Mathar's day

△ During school recess, Mathar and his friends talk and play in the playground.

Swimming

"I like going swimming with Nusrat and Tom. I can swim really fast, and Nusrat and I sometimes race each other across the pool."

Mathar is woken up every morning by his vibrating alarm clock. Mathar knows his way around his house and feels his way to the bathroom. Then he chooses what to wear for school. Mathar keeps his clothes in one place, so he knows exactly where everything is. Although Mathar can't see shapes very well, he can see colors. He finds the sweater he wants to wear by looking at the color and feeling the texture. After breakfast, a taxi takes Mathar to school.

At school, there is an assistant named Miss Seagrove who stays with Mathar all day. Mathar takes classes like everyone else. He uses a talking computer and a machine that prints Braille. Miss Seagrove sits next to him and helps him when he needs it. Mathar wears a hearing aid because he can't hear very well. Mathar's class teacher, Mr. Wright, wears a microphone around his neck that he speaks into. The microphone is connected to Mathar's hearing aid. Mathar does all his schoolwork in Braille. Then Miss Seagrove puts it into ordinary writing for Mr. Wright to mark. Mr. Wright sticks raised paper blobs on Mathar's exercise book so Mathar knows where he has made mistakes.

▽ Mathar uses his fingers to read a book written in Braille.

At recess, Mathar goes outside with his friends. They like to play football using a special ball with a bell inside so that Mathar can easily tell where the ball is.

At home, Mathar likes to surf the Internet on his talking computer. Sometimes Mathar, Nusrat, and Tom go swimming with their mother. Mathar also likes reading. He gets books in Braille from a library for blind people. His favorite books are about science. When he grows up, Mathar would like to be a scientist so that he can work on some of the interesting things he's read about.

Lucy goes shopping

On Saturday afternoons, Lucy likes to go shopping at the local mall with her best friend Sophie. They have been there together many times before, so Lucy knows the way. Even so, she has to concentrate very hard.

Lucy loves walking down the street to the bus stop. She holds a long white cane when she walks. The cane helps Lucy feel bumps in the sidewalk. She has walked this route many times and knows it well. The bus stop is right beside the bakery, where there is a nice smell.

▽ Lucy likes to have Sophie with her to give her advice when shopping for clothes.

Lucy and Sophie like shopping for clothes best. Lucy can feel the clothes, and Sophie tells her what color they are. Last Saturday, Lucy bought a new pair of pants. She tried them on, and Sophie told her how she looked. Then, Lucy took them to the cashier and paid for them. When Lucy goes home, her mother will sew a shaped button inside her new pants so she can tell them from other pairs of pants.

△ Lucy and Sophie relax when they have finished shopping.

After looking around all the stores, Lucy and Sophie usually go for soda and a pizza. Sophie carries the tray and pays the bill, because Lucy has her cane and her shopping. Once when Lucy was waiting for Sophie to pay the bill, someone started to pull her toward the door. Lucy felt very worried, even though she knew Sophie could see her. She said, "No thank you, I'm waiting for my friend," and the person let her go.

Ask before you help

"I know I sometimes need help from a sighted person, but I wish people would ask me if there is anything they can do before they pull my arm."

Katie and Teddy

On the days when she works, Katie takes the bus into town with her guide dog, Teddy. Katie used a white cane before Katie got Teddy, but she found it more difficult to get to work. Some people didn't see her cane and tripped over it or walked into it, so she decided to have a guide dog. She and Teddy had to do some training to get used to each other and learn how to work together. While Katie is at work, Teddy lies beside her desk. Teddy guides Katie if she has to go to another part of the building. Katie uses commands, such as "Sit" and "Forward," to tell Teddy what to do.

At work, Katie has many jobs to do as a receptionist, and she's very busy. She types letters on her computer, which has large print on the screen so she can see what she's written. When someone comes to visit the office for a meeting, Katie takes the visitor's name and phones the person he or she is going to see.

▷ When Teddy has her harness on, she knows she has to guide Katie. While Katie is working, Teddy can relax.

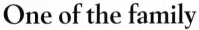

◁ Katie and Mike go walking with Teddy on weekends.

One of the family

"Teddy is one of the family now. She helps me lead a normal life just like everybody else."

On weekends, Katie and Teddy sometimes walk down to the local stores. Many people in the stores know Teddy. They like to stop and say hello to Katie and Teddy.

Katie's blindness doesn't keep her from doing active things. She and her husband, Mike, go to a dancing class twice a week. They like Latin-American dancing best. On weekends, they often go walking in the park or in the country. They take Teddy with them; the dog loves to have a free run without wearing a harness. Teddy wears a collar with a bell so Katie can hear where she is. Katie and Mike love traveling to different countries. This year, she and Mike are going to Greece with their children, Sarah and Dominic.

Blindness and everyday life

◁ These blind children are playing together in an adventure playground.

Blind people use the sight they have got to help them go about their everyday lives. The other senses such as feeling, hearing, and smelling are also important. But blind people don't have better senses than other people. In fact, some blind people like Mathar are hearing-impaired as well as blind.

Blind people may need to learn special skills to help them do things. When Lucy first went into town, a mobility instructor from her local agency for the blind took her on the bus until she was familiar with the route. Her friends realize she needs help sometimes, and Lucy knows she can call on them when she needs to.

When people who used to be able to see lose their sight, like Katie, they have to learn to do things they used to do before they become blind. This may involve learning things sighted people take for granted, such as making a cup of coffee or getting around safely in the street. The process of learning to cope with daily life as a blind person is called rehabilitation.

There are a number of aids and devices that help make everyday activities easier. Like Lucy and Mathar, many blind people use a white cane to help them get around. Some blind people, like Katie, have a guide dog. When people see someone with a white cane or a guide dog, it lets them know that the person is blind. People should never pet a working guide dog, because the dog needs to concentrate on guiding the blind person.

◁ Lucy's white cane helps her get around and lets people know that she is blind.

◁ This partially sighted woman is using a computer that enlarges print to make it big and clear enough for her to see.

△ This is Braille. The letters are made of raised dots so blind people can feel them to read.

In some buildings, there are Braille signs on doors and inside elevators to help blind people know where they are. Asking sighted people for directions and using a long cane or a guide dog help a blind person find his or her way around an unfamiliar environment. Recorded announcements tell blind people when trains and buses reach their stop.

Large print, such as on signs, notices, Internet sites, and books, helps greatly. Buildings should also have good lighting. Most people find it difficult to see clearly in dark, dimly lit places.

Other things that can help blind people are lights at pedestrian crossings that make a beeping sound when it is safe to cross the road. In unfamiliar places, a blind person can use a tactile map and even a tactile compass to help find his or her way around.

Many gadgets for use in the house, such as talking kitchen scales, talking recipes, and easy-to-see clock timers, are available. At school and work, talking computers, calculators, tactile rulers, telephones with large print keypads, and many other aids can help people who have lost most or all of their sight.

▽ This gadget keeps hot drinks from spilling over the top of a mug or cup by beeping when the water reaches the right level.

Is there a cure for blindness?

In most cases, there is no cure for total blindness. Scientists and doctors are trying to find out more so that in the future they may be able to prevent loss of sight and find new ways to treat it. Some scientists are studying the way people can inherit conditions that cause blindness. Other scientists are also looking at ways to replace damaged cells in the retina with new ones. This would help people with some kinds of blindness be able to see again.

▽ Scientists are working to discover what causes blindness and to try and find new ways to treat it.

△ You should always take care to protect your eyes from accident or injury. For example, wear goggles in science classes.

It is likely to be a long time before scientists understand all the causes of blindness and how to prevent them. However, there are some things that can be done to help prevent sight loss. Some children and adults lose their sight in accidents, so it is always important to protect your eyes by using a mask or goggles when playing sports or working with dangerous tools such as electric drills. For example, if you don't wear a mask while drilling, a bit of grit or wood could fly into your eye and cause a lot of damage.

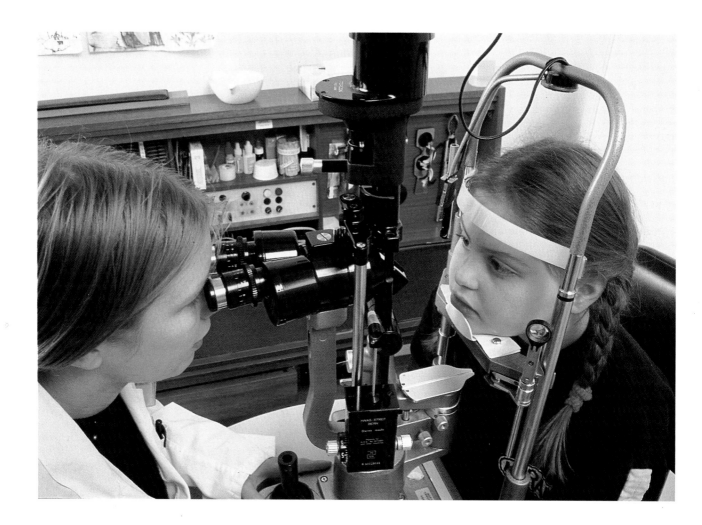

△ This girl is having her eyes tested by an optometrist.

Some people lose their sight through disease or an infection. For example, people who wear contact lenses should always clean them very carefully to avoid developing an infection. Both children and adults should have regular eye tests to check whether eyesight problems are developing. Some eye conditions such as glaucoma can develop slowly. Regular eye tests can detect fluid pressure building up in the eyeball. People can then have treatment such as laser treatment and eyedrops to prevent damage to the optic nerve before it causes blindness.

Cataracts are a visual impairment that are reversible. They can be treated by surgery. However, in many poor countries where cataracts are common, there is not enough money for everyone who needs an operation to have one.

Everyone should have eye tests regularly. They help people discover any infections early and get the right treatment before the infection can increase. Eye tests also show people whether they need to wear glasses. Wearing glasses prevents eye strain and makes life easier.

▽ This boy is having his eyes checked by his doctor.

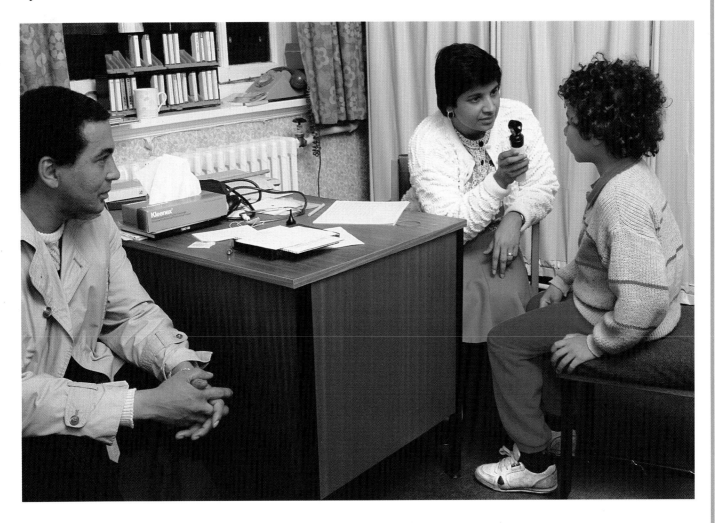

Looking to the future

Mathar, Lucy, and Katie are just like you, except that they are visually impaired or blind. Blind people can do most of the things that sighted people can do; they can go to school and college. Mathar, Lucy, and Katie enjoy spending time with their friends, going on vacations, having hobbies, and playing sports.

◁ Like many other teenagers, Lucy enjoys playing her guitar.

Blind people come from all sorts of families and backgrounds and live all sorts of lives. There are blind sportspeople, gardeners, artists, writers, teachers, journalists, engineers, social workers, computer programmers, and lawyers—to name just a few.

△ Katie enjoys having a drink with her best friend.

Mathar, Lucy, and Katie do not allow their blindness to keep them from doing what they enjoy. But life is not always easy. Sometimes other people do not give them the chance to do what they like to do, and this upsets them. Like most people, they do not ask you to feel sorry for them. They want you to accept them and sometimes to help them so that they can get on with their lives.

Getting help

◁ With a bit of thought, people who can see can help make life easier for blind people. For example, web sites on the Internet would be more useful for blind people if larger type were used.

Children or adults who are blind don't want you to treat them any differently from the way you treat people who can see. However, they may sometimes need your help, so if you see a blind person who is looking unsure don't be afraid to approach. If you ask whether you can help and a blind person says "No," don't be offended. Not all blind people need help, but you won't know unless you ask.

There are many organizations that assist blind people. Some of them provide help and advice on all aspects of blindness. Some provide information on services in a particular town, city, or area. You can find details of these from the library or the Yellow Pages telephone directory. Some organizations specialize in helping people whose blindness is caused by a particular eye condition.

American Foundation for the Blind (AFB), 11 Pennsylvania Plaza, Suite 300, New York, NY 10001. (800) 232-5463. Their web site is at http://www.afb.org. This organization collects and provides information about blindness. It publishes books, pamphlets, and videos. It has the world's largest collection of print materials on blindness.

△ Many organizations publish magazines, books, and leaflets in Braille.

National Association for Parents of the Visually Impaired, Inc. (NAPVI), P.O. Box 317, Watertown, MA 02471. (800) 562-6265. Their web site is at http://spedex.com/napvi. NAPVI has information for parents with blind and visually impaired children. It publishes a newsletter, pamphlets, and books. NAPVI holds conferences and provides training and support for parents.

National Federation of the Blind (FNFB), 1800 Johnson Street, Baltimore, MD 21230. (410) 659-9314. Their web site is at http://www.nfb.org. The largest organization of blind persons in the United States, NFB helps blind persons achieve self-confidence, self-respect, and integration into society. NFB offers scholarships, help with special technology, and job information.

Prevent Blindness America, 500 East Remington Road, Schaumburg, IL 60173. (800) 221-3004. Their web site is at http://www.preventblindness.org. The nation's leading volunteer eye health and safety organization.

Glossary

Braille A language for blind people. The letters are made of raised dots.

Cells Very small parts of any living creature—animal or human. Your skin, your eyes, your heart, in fact, every part of your body is made up of groups of cells.

Contact lenses Curved pieces of tissue in the eye that help us focus. Lenses made from plastic or glass are used to help correct people's eyesight if they can't see very well.

Cornea The clear front part of the eye. Light first enters the eye through the cornea.

Diabetes A disease in which the body is unable to turn food into energy. People with diabetes can develop a blinding disease called diabetic retinopathy.

Inherited Things that have been transferred, such as the color of eyes and hair, or certain diseases, from one family member to another.

Learning disabilities People with learning disabilities often learn to do things more slowly than other people and need some extra help.

Malnourishment When someone does not have enough food to stay healthy or when the food is not digested properly because of a fault in the digestion or disease. Malnourishment is a common cause of blindness in poor countries.

Mobility officer Someone who helps blind people get to know their surroundings.

Optic nerve A bundle of fibers that carries messages from the retina to the brain.

Optometrist Someone who detects sight conditions and advises people whether they should wear glasses or contact lenses.

Retina The tissue at the back of the eye. It is connected to the brain by the optic nerve.

Senses The ways in which our bodies get information about the world around us. There are five senses: seeing, hearing, touching, tasting, and smelling.

Tactile Having to do with the sense of touch.

Tissue A collection of cells. The skin is a tissue.

Ultraviolet light Harmful ultraviolet light from the sun.

Further information

BOOKS

Alexander, Sally H. *Mom's Best Friend*. Old Tappan, NJ: Simon & Schuster Children's Books, 1992.

———. *Taking Hold: My Journey Into Blindness*. Old Tappan, NJ: Simon & Schuster Children's Books, 1994.

Freedman, Russell. *Out of Darkness: The Story of Louis Braille*. New York: Dutton Children's Books, 1997.

Hunter, Edith F. *Child of the Silent Night: The Story of Laura Bridgman*. New York: William Morrow & Co., 1999.

Ring, Elizabeth. *Assistance Dogs: In Special Service*. Brookfield, CT: Millbrook Press, 1993.

MAGAZINES

Blind children can get regular print magazines in large print and on tape, e.g., *Cricket*, *National Geographic World*, and *Sports Illustrated for Kids*.

VIDEOS

The following videos are all available from American Federation for the Blind:

Helen Keller in Her Story. Helen Keller was a famous deaf and blind woman. This video is about her life, her teacher, and her friend.

Not Without Sight. This video discusses eye conditions and shows what visually impaired people see.

What Do You Do When You See a Blind Person? This is a funny video about how to act around blind people.

Oh, I See. This video shows how blind and visually impaired students do things at school.

Index

Numbers in **bold** refer to pictures as well as text.